QUIET KID

written and illustrated by
Debbie Fox

ISBN-13: 978-1478210061

ISBN-10: 1478210060

A little boat is far from shore
floating on an empty sea.
Never knowing what's in store,
it's strong and silent, just like me.

I am a quiet kid you might know
in a world that's fast and loud.
It's hard to let my feelings show
within the many of a crowd.

We are the hang back kids, and so
at the playground's edge you'll see us.
Joining in takes time, we take it slow -
that's how it is to be us.

I'm a curious kid, reflective,
in a world where thoughts can scatter.
I look closely, like a detective,
at how things work and why they matter.

We are the classroom thinkers who
work hard and pay attention,
but sometimes our minds can wander to
worlds of our own invention.

Quiet kids make fantastic friends
who don't gossip, brag or yell.
It's a quiet friend who naturally tends
to listen really well.

Like a jet plane with cool, awesome powers,
sometimes I'm just pure energy ...
and did you know I can talk for hours
with close friends and family?

Animals can growl or squeak or squawk,
be silent or be roaring;
if they all shared just one creature talk,
nature would be so boring.

This world would be one noisy place
and we'd find it rather shocking,
if every mouth on every face
was non-stop talk - talk - talking!

Differences should be respected
and not seen as bad or as wrong.
All kids want to feel accepted
and know for sure that they belong.

We were born quiet kids as we should be,
and there are lots of us to be found.
Don't need to change - why would we?
We're the most interesting kids around.

Quiet kids have the patience for wondering,
we're creative and thoughtful as well.
Our brains are not quiet - they're thundering!
I like me as I am, you can tell.

Many kinds of boats that fill the sea
are sailing the same waters, differently.
Some do their best sailing quietly -
strong and silent and just like me.

If YOU are a Quiet Kid ...

I have been dreaming up this book for a long time now because I think you deserve a book that shows how interesting and awesome you are. Quiet kids are part of a special group of people known as **introverts**. Introverted kids grow up to be introverted grown-ups, and I know this for sure because I am one!

We are folks who usually find and get our best energy from *inside ourselves* - too much noise and activity is kind of tiring to us. Introverts really like some alone time to dream up ideas and explore things that interest us. All of this 'brain time' can make us very creative and thoughtful people. We can talk A LOT when we're with a close friend or our family - especially about things we really like. But it does take us a little more time to get to know others and try new things, and we like to think it through before we speak. Of course, this doesn't mean we don't like to be a little wild and silly sometimes, too.

There are more people who are known as **extroverts**. You know many of them at school; maybe some right in your own family. Extroverts usually get their best energy from *outside themselves*. They love noise, group activities and lots of attention; they might find being by themselves kind of boring. Kids like this might be really popular and have lots of friends, but that doesn't make them better or kinder or more successful people.

Sometimes you might feel like you're a little 'different' than the other kids. It's okay to feel that way, but you need to know that the world is filled with lots of fantastic introverts. Some of your favorite actors, writers, athletes and musicians are introverts and they probably felt a little different when they were kids, too. What's really important is to accept and respect all people for the way they are, including yourself. Being a quiet kid - it's just the way that you are, and it's a great way to be.

ABOUT THE AUTHOR

Debbie Fox is an elementary school arts and literacy educator
and has created innovative, award-winning programs for children.
The daughter of two introverted commercial artists,
she grew up a quiet kid in noisy New York.
Debbie could always find her voice through her art, and
graduated from the Ontario College of Art in Toronto, Canada.
Debbie is passionate about giving young people
creative opportunities to express themselves.

She and her husband live in Florida, close to their grown
children. This is her fourth illustrated children's book.

Good-Bye Bully Machine

written by Debbie Fox and Allan L. Beane, Ph.D.
illustrated by Debbie Fox

Book and companion card game published by Free Spirit Publishing.

From the Publisher's website:
"Kids learn what bullying is, why it hurts, and what they can do to end it with this fresh, compelling book. With its contemporary collage art, lively layout, and straightforward text, *Good-Bye Bully Machine* engages kids and keeps them turning pages.

"The unique format of *Good-Bye Bully Machine* helps kids understand the definition and impact of bullying by comparing it to a mean machine - the Bully Machine. Kids can see how bullying makes the machine grow more imposing, while kind behaviors dismantle it.

"Through the machine, kids gain awareness of their role in bullying, whether they are targets, bullies, bystanders - or all three. The role of the bystander is especially important. *Good-Bye Bully Machine* helps kids see the power of the bystander to become an ally which means learning to show empathy, engage in kind acts, and take a stand against bullying. It's a perfect way to engage reluctant readers and hard-to-reach kids."

Made in the USA
San Bernardino, CA
08 April 2016